J.A. x J.M. Stor

Christmas

# SHIPSIDES'
*~ Bristol ~*

# SHIPSIDES'
## *~ Bristol ~*

TEXT BY
**ROBERT WALL**

**HALSGROVE**

In association with
**ALEXANDER
GALLERY**
FINE ART DEALERS

First published in 2001 by Halsgrove
Images © 2001 Frank Shipsides
Text © 2001 Robert Wall

**British Library Cataloguing-in-Publication Data**
A CIP record for this title is available from the British Library


ISBN 1 84114 132 1


**HALSGROVE**
Publishing, Media and Distribution

Halsgrove House
Lower Moor Way
Tiverton, Devon EX16 6SS
Tel: 01884 243242
Fax: 01884 243325
email sales@halsgrove.com
website www.halsgrove.com


Printed and bound in Italy by Centro Grafico Ambrosiano, Milan

*Dedicated to the memory of my dear wife*
*Phyl Shipsides*
*whose never-ending and devoted support encouraged*
*my efforts to paint the Bristol scene, a city we both grew to love.*

# The City and County of Bristol

## AN INTRODUCTION

Bristol is unique among the large cities of England as the only one to enjoy a long history dating back to the beginning of the last millennium, circa 1000 AD. Cities like Birmingham, Manchester, Liverpool and Leeds all date their growth into major conurbations from the Industrial Revolution of the mid-eighteenth century and their history suffers accordingly. Bristol, on the other hand, was England's second city for over eight hundred years. Its rich political, economic and architectural history adds much to the atmosphere that today inspires pride in the resident and attracts visitors by the thousand.

Bristol grew up on a small peninsula that lies between the rivers Avon and Frome, a few miles inland from the Severn estuary and where contemporary engineers felt able to bridge the Avon. The first evidence of the city's existence is found on coins minted in the reign of Ethelred the Unrede (978–1016) at Bricgstowe, in Anglo-Saxon 'the place of the bridge'. There is abundant evidence of ancient British and Roman settlements around the site that was to become Bristol but it seems that a sizeable town only began to spring up in the reign of Alfred the Great (871-891). Here on the tidal, muddy banks of the river, ships could lie safely to be unloaded. The Anglo-Saxon Chronicle first mentions Bristol in 1051 when it records travels to Ireland, where an immigrant Viking community was among the first clients of early Bristol merchants. The bridge, from which the town took its name, was probably a wooden one (traces of wooden piers were found when the present Bristol Bridge was built in 1768) and the merchants built their houses on the eastern bank of the Avon in the pleasant meadows of Redcliffe. If one wonders why the town was built so far from the sea, along 6 miles of difficult river, the answer lies in the ease with which the site could be fortified and the fact that technology was insufficiently advanced to allow a bridge of greater size further downstream.

By the time of the Norman Conquest in 1066, Bristol was probably inhabited by up to 15,000 people, a statistic that was to remain throughout the Middle Ages, making Bristol England's second city until the late eighteenth century. Bristolians had offered no resistance to William the Conqueror, probably welcoming his firm rule under which they could return to their main preoccupation – trade. Nevertheless, King William banned the Bristol merchants from what to the popular mind was their staple trade – slaving. He ordered the construction of a large castle on the eastern side of the town. The slave trade was mainly with Ireland and the Bristolians were not above kidnapping any unfortunates they could lay their hands on. The trade was allowed to restart during the civil war in the reign of King Stephen (1135–1154). Bristol declared for the pretender Queen Maud, who made the city her base, bringing with her Henry, her son. When Stephen died in 1154, Maud's son, still only twenty one, took the throne as Henry II, who many historians would later identify, with Elizabeth I, as one of the two greatest rulers that England was to have. Henry's first act was to grant Bristol a valuable charter in 1155. This document established the city's prosperity which was to last throughout the Middle Ages. The early layout of the city grew around the crossroads of four streets that still exist – Wine Street, Broad Street, Corn Street and High Street – and the bridge where High Street ended in the later St Nicholas Gate which together with the castle were to set the pattern of the city for the next six centuries. Here, above the bridge, the ships came and went. Exports of wool and imports of Baltic timber appear to have been the staple trades, to which the charter of Henry II also adds wine, hides, corn, cheese and iron.

So Bristol prospered, adopting a shrewd loyalty to the ruling Plantagenet kings, and escaping the worst effects of the Wars of the Roses by pacifying each side in turn. William Canynges (born c.1399) was the grandson of a merchant of the same name who commenced the rebuilding of St Mary Redcliffe Church in the preceding century. The younger Canynges shared his grandfather's love of the great church and spent much of his trading profit in its restoration. He is typical of the merchants whose wealth and power made them major players in Bristol. He was also Mayor five times and in 1467 delegated some of the port administration powers to the Fraternity of Merchants and Mariners of Bristol. In this year the records of the Society of Merchant Venturers begin.

So the stage was set for the Age of Discovery, as the latter years of the fifteenth century were to be called by future historians. The Wars of the Roses had ended in 1485 at Bosworth with victory for the careful Henry VII who founded the Tudor dynasty and was determined on peace. His way of achieving it was to encourage trade, which happened to coincide with a growing interest of the Bristol merchants in trading with lands widely believed to lie across the western ocean. Bristol had long traded in dried cod from Iceland and here the sailors from the Avon would have heard of fabled Vinland which the Norse sagas said lay to the south-west.

By the time Henry VII was on the throne, several Bristol expeditions westward had been attempted but with no reported success. Another unproved story is a visit to Bristol in 1477 of the young Christopher Columbus, eager to take passage westward in a Bristol ship.

To a Geonese, domiciled in Bristol, went the honour of eventual success. Cabot came to Bristol by way of Venice and settled in the city in the 1490s. He seems to have been well received, for he was a leading citizen in five years, and on 5 March, 1496, secured letters patent from the King, authorising a voyage to 'sail to all parts, countries and seas of the east, of the west and of the north…' Although there is limited evidence that Bristol ships had sighted the New World years before Columbus while on fishing voyages to the Newfoundland Banks, we are certain that Cabot sighted the mainland of North America on 24 June, 1497, the first European in modern history to do so. He had left Bristol on 2 May with his son Sebastian and a crew of 20 in the ship *Matthew* of 50 tons. There is no evidence to pinpoint the landing place and it could have been anywhere from Maine to Labrador. Newfoundland has been the popular choice of Bristol historians. The Cabots (for history credits both father and son with the voyage) returned to Bristol in triumph on 6 August, 1497. Cabot was now an important national figure and immediately set about preparing a future voyage. From this, in 1498, he did not return and was apparently lost at sea.

Where one Bristol ship could go, others could follow and there were several voyages from Bristol to America up to 1508–9, when the new King Henry VIII discouraged any exploration which would upset Spain, his wife being a princess of that country. Therefore the early voyages of discovery did not profit Bristol a great deal and there was little done by Englishmen in the first half of the sixteenth century to follow up Cabot's initiative. Nevertheless, the door was open and the great days of the

Elizabethans were at hand. In the time of Cabot, the Collector of Customs of the Port of Bristol was one Richard ap Meryck, or Ameryck. Staunchly, Bristolians claim that Cabot called his discovery America in the Collector's honour. It may well be so.

The years of the reigns of the intermediate Tudor monarchs were ones of indifferent success for Bristol, but the arrival of Elizabeth I on the throne introduced an era of prosperity that is still celebrated in the city as 'the golden days of good Queen Bess'. Elizabeth had a shrewd talent for winning the hearts and minds of her people and Bristolians adored her. Not so the Stuarts who soon fell out with Bristol to the extent that in 1631 Charles I went so far as to ban the tobacco trade in his search for tax revenues. The bitter war between King and Parliament opened in 1642. It was essentially a land war as most civil fights are, and the story of Bristol's adherence to Parliament, its capture by Prince Rupert in July, 1643, and his subsequent loss of his prize to Fairfax and Cromwell in September 1645, have all been well recorded. During the Royalist occupation, the trade of the city all but disappeared and a decade of hard work during the Commonwealth was needed for its recovery. By the time of the Restoration of Charles II in 1660, Bristol was prosperous again. In the eyes of Samuel Pepys, who visited in 1668, the port appeared a 'large and noble place'.

Bristol was held for the King during the Monmouth rising in June 1685 against James II. Three years later, in 1688 the city promptly declared for William of Orange and the flight of James II marked the end of the old Bristol. True the city was much the same as ever, largely enclosed in its walls, but the castle, symbol of so much strife and repression, had been demolished in 1655 and its fall coincided with the birth of new ideas about social justice. The men of Bristol had taken these ideas with them to the colonies in the New World and would eventually develop the passion for freedom that inspired Washington's armies and led to the foundation of the United States.

At the beginning of the eighteenth century, Bristol entered what some writers have described as her Golden Age. The phrase is an apt one, for in no previous time in her history had the wealth of her citizens been so extensive. She was the country's leading port after London and would remain so for most of the century. Her population was up to 20,000 in 1700 and would grow another 44,000 by the century's end. The remains of eighteenth century expansion can be seen in Bristol today in such buildings as the Corn Exchange, the houses of Orchard Street and St Thomas Church. Park Street was laid out and on the Marsh, behind the quays and shipyards, the well ordered grace of Queen Square took shape to become one of Bristol's glories. As the century ended, Clifton had started the climb along her gorge that was to lift the suburb to the heights of Georgian elegance.

Meanwhile the traditional trades with Ireland, France, Spain and the Baltic continued. To these were added rum, sugar and tobacco from the Americas and also the controversial and loathsome slaving. Bristol merchants had been aware of the possibilities of the trade for decades as there was a huge demand for labour in the plantations of the Americas. The Dutch were supplying the colonists as early as the time of the Civil War. The fight of the Society of Merchant Venturers for a share of the slave trade went on for over half a century, until the trade was regulated in 1750 and Bristol became a full partner. Despite all her complaints, Bristol grew rich on the slave trade. In the first decade of the eighteenth century, an average of 50 ships a year sailed from the city to the Guinea coast and in 1725, Bristol ships carried 16,950 slaves to American ports. Nevertheless, the figures over the century as a whole show that London and Liverpool were far greater slavers than Bristol ever was. As an example, from 1795–1804, Bristol transported 10,718 negro slaves, while London's total was 46,405 and Liverpool's an incredible 332,800! Meanwhile, William Wilberforce's abolition campaign was gathering momentum. He succeeded in 1807.

By then, the decline in Bristol's trade which was to last through the nineteenth century had set in. Bristol had been overtaken by Liverpool as the second port of Britain and the size of ships had grown to a point where it was impossibly dangerous for them to use the Avon. This threat of ever larger ships would loom again in 1890 and 1960! So, in 1802 a scheme was commissioned from the leading engineer William Jessop that was substantially the form of the present Floating Harbour. A Bill to float the Bristol Dock Company was promoted and work commenced on 1 May, 1804. The scheme included a large new locked entrance named after the Duke of Cumberland, a new cut for the River Avon, three dams, a feeder canal and Bath and Bedminster bridges. Water was first let into the New Cut in January, 1809. Bristol had her first modern port and it was now up to her to use it.

This was difficult as the dock had far exceeded the planned cost. Port charges soared to become the highest in the country and trade fell away. To overcome some of these problems, the Dock Company engaged the services of a young engineer, Isambard Kingdom Brunel and soon found they had a genius on their hands. The schemes devised by Brunel in the first half of the nineteenth century had a great impact on Bristol and created much of the modern reputation of the city. In 1832, Brunel won the competition to design the Clifton Suspension Bridge, which was to become the city's trademark. In 1833, he was appointed engineer to the Great Western Railway and much of his railbed is still in use. Five years later in April, 1838, his steamer *Great Western* set out from Bristol to become the first Atlantic liner to offer a regular service and in 1843, he launched the iron monster *Great Britain* which set standards of ship construction for decades to come. After a varied career she remains preserved in Bristol to this day.

The late nineteenth century saw Bristol expand both north and south, and east along the Avon valley as the suburbs of Horfield, Bedminster, St George and Kingswood grew to house the ever increasing numbers of workers needed by the new industries. Among these were Fry's chocolate and Wills' tobacco. Tobacco had been coming into Bristol for centuries and by 1660 accounted for a third of the city's trade. But W.D. & H.O. Wills turned the trade into a basic industry which lasted until almost the twenty-first century and did much to create the University of Bristol. A new dock for larger ships was opened at Avonmouth in 1877 and was again expanded in 1902–08 to create the Royal Edward Dock. This served the port through two world wars and after, until the huge new Royal Portbury Dock was opened on the south bank of the Avon in 1977.

The other major development of the twentieth century in Bristol was Bristol tramway magnate Sir George White's establishment of a thriving aircraft business in the north Bristol suburb of Filton. This provided thousands of Bristol families with jobs for life, supplied weapons of war in two conflicts and led to the development of the great supersonic aircraft Concorde.

Commerce and industry are the main themes of the Bristol story. They remain so today, as the thousand year story of the city continues to unwind, and her citizens continue to create new visions for the future. In this book, Frank Shipsides has set out a wonderful series of images of this vital and challenging city. Long may it prosper.

*Frank Shipsides*

# Frank Shipsides – Portrait of the Artist

Not far from the centre of Bristol, on the slopes of St Michael's Hill, stands the home of an old Bristol society. A converted tithe barn, it is known somewhat idiosyncratically as the Wigwam and it will come as no surprise that this same Wigwam is inhabited by savages, in this case the Bristol Savages, one of the oldest artist's societies of its kind in the kingdom.

Ever since it emerged as one of England's great trading centres at the beginning of the eighteenth century, Bristol has cherished an artistic tradition, much of it devoted to marine art. It was here that Nicholas Pocock lived, who was to become first a master mariner and then the father of modern British maritime art. In the nineteenth century, Francis Danby and Samuel Jackson carried on the Bristol artistic tradition. William Muller spent some time here, and the great Victorian maritime artist, Joseph Walter, spent his entire career in Bristol, working from his studio in Temple Street.

In the early years of the twentieth century, Arthur Wilde Parsons carried on the tradition which Frank Shipsides maintains today.

Frank Winston Shipsides was born in the Nottinghamshire town of Mansfield, where his father worked in the hosiery business. The family name is unusual and seems particularly appropriate for someone so skilled in the presentation of maritime affairs on canvas. The family is said to have originated in the famous Nottinghamshire village of Gotham, of 'Wise men' notoriety. The young Shipsides grew up in an artistic atmosphere. His father was a skilled musician and his elder sister was keenly interested in all forms of art. Nevertheless, Frank Shipsides' training was to be in the practical form of a seven-year apprenticeship with the printing and publishing company Barringer, Wallis and Manners.

Years later, Shipsides wrote, 'It was not terribly skilled work to begin with. The most artistic thing I did in those early days was to dust down the potted palms and busts on plinths which were used to give added tone to the studio.'

The budding artist was just fourteen years old and received his formal training by attending art classes at night school. Later he wrote, 'We had a good grounding in the business. The studio manager looked after his apprentices and, of course, we could look forward to earning at least £4 a week when we were indentured, which was a lot more than most working men in those days.'

Following his apprenticeship, Frank spent a number of years with an offset process company in Nottingham. The particular expertise of this organisation was the proofing of brochures, catalogues and showcards, the nuts and bolts of the whole publishing business. Again to quote from his own words, 'We worked like hell. If you wanted to leave early, say at eight o'clock in the evening, you'd slip down the back stairs in case old Toddy saw you. At ten or eleven at night, one of the kids would be waiting with a barrow while you were getting the last colour on, so he could rush the proofs to the last train to London or wherever the work was going'

It was at this time, after he had been with the offset process company for about seven years, that he met and married his wife Phyllis, a Mansfield girl who had been born almost alongside the centre tree of Sherwood Forest. In due course they had two children, daughter Jennifer and son Patrick. With art running so firmly in the blood of the family, it is no surprise to learn that Jennifer first worked as a restorer with Frost and Reed, then the

National Trust, while Patrick is a technical illustrator and an able painter of marine subjects.

Frank Shipsides' true love, however, is of ships and the sea and it was this desire to be nearer shipping that eventually brought him to Bristol. At the time, Bristol was a great centre of the printing industry, with E. S. & A. Robinson and Mardon, Son and Hall leading the substantial industry located in the city. Frank joined the printing firm Bennetts but the outbreak of war found him moving into the engineering industry where he worked as a draughtsman on wartime production. In these years his love affair with Bristol began. He was painting more and more on his own account and began to acquire that knowledge of Bristol ships and shipping along with the port of Bristol, that was to show in such great detail in his later work. After the war, in 1948 he moved to Mardon, Son and Hall where he worked as a senior artist for more than twenty years. He then went freelance, at which time a chance meeting with Jim Fardon, a partner of Bristol's well known Alexander Gallery, led to Fardon suggesting that Shipsides' work was certainly worth a one man show. When it took place on 30 November 1972, it was an immediate sell-out.

Shipsides records, 'I owe Alexander Gallery a great debt. I remember doing a particular painting of that scene that everyone loves in Bristol, St Mary Redcliffe church looking up from Prince Street Bridge in a morning light, the spire silhouetted against the yellow sky. I remember Jim asking me what I thought it might fetch. I mentioned a figure only to be told to my surprise that two people had already offered to buy it at a price of nearly three times what I thought it was worth!'

That one man show in November, 1972 consisted of oil and watercolour paintings of marine subjects, among which tall ships featured in numbers, but also contained a number of landscapes of Bristol which showed clearly the artist's love of the city.

Since that first show in 1972, eight others have followed. These days a Shipsides' preview is a great Bristol occasion, usually with the Lord Mayor in attendance. A queue of eager, would-be purchasers forms at the doors of the gallery long before the show opens. Frank Shipsides is a delightfully modest man and all his success makes it even harder for one to obtain his views on painting. He has, however, recorded that, 'oil enables one to put more depth into a picture but I enjoy the discipline of working in watercolour. One cannot afford to make mistakes. Watercolour is a delicate art, greatly underrated in my view. Composition seems to take care of itself if you have found the right spot. I remember one occasion in Belgium when I spent a lot of time choosing just the right viewpoint. A passer-by pointed out, while talking about the work in progress, that Winston Churchill had once painted from that very spot. I was not surprised. Any good artist with a natural feel for composition would have come to the same conclusion.'

He is not a great enthusiast for still life. To quote him again, 'It is difficult for me to get worked up about a bag of Mother's Pride, but Corn Street in silvery evening light, now that's a different matter. Or a rusty old tramp steamer, a bit scruffy to look at but

full of character and romance. When I paint an old ship, it's not just what the eye sees but also what I feel about her.' His enthusiasm for large square rig sailing vessels and his precise knowledge of those very complicated sailing machines has allowed him to produce finished ship paintings which, while they look authentic because they are so accurate, nevertheless have the smell of the sea and the creak of rigging emanating from them. He is also a very experienced ship model-maker and his works have been displayed in Bristol City Museum, London and Stockholm where they have been awarded silver and bronze medals.

By the late 1970s, Frank Shipsides was an established West Country artist with a considerable following and it was at that time that he moved into a new field. He produced a book about Bristol which contained well over 50 drawings. Published as *Bristol Impressions*, it was an immediate success and was followed in 1979 by *Bristol: Profile of a City* which also sold well. Two years later, in 1981, in collaboration with Robert Wall, he produced *Bristol: Maritime City*, a history of Bristol's long maritime tradition illustrated in colour and line drawings. A fourth book, *Frank Shipsides' Bristol*, followed in 1984.

Since then, Frank Shipsides has pursued the busy career of a recognised major artist. Limited editions of reproductions of subjects both in Bristol and London are familiar sights in both cities. He exhibits annually at the Bristol Savages and other prestigious exhibitions. In 1983, to honour the warship H.M.S. *Bristol*, the City Council commissioned him to paint seven large canvases of the ships that have borne the name of the city, commencing with a warship built by Oliver Cromwell and ending with the current holder of the name. Shipsides responded to the challenge with characteristic passion and the seven canvasses now hang in the entrance hall to the Council House. Further municipal commissions followed. Near the H.M.S. *Bristol* collection hangs a Shipsides impression on canvas of John Cabot's ship *Matthew*, which sailed from Bristol in 1497 to discover the mainland of North America, and which voyage the replica *Matthew* repeated in 1997. He was also the artist requested to record on canvas the various visits of Her Majesty Queen Elizabeth II to Bristol. Another interest, the creation of scenery for the Bristol Catholic Players Savoy Operas, led to a medal award from the Vatican. In July, 1989 the University of Bristol conferred the honorary degree of Master of Arts on Frank Shipsides, a well-merited honour. A notable landmark for the Shipsides family came in July 2000, when Frank, together with his son and daughter-in-law, Anna

and his daughter Jenny Thwaites were the four artists featured in a successful exhibition held on Clevedon Pier.

Today Frank Shipsides remains a busy working artist. His style continues to develop and much of his recent work will rival that of William Wyllie and Charles Dixon for atmosphere, detail and the capacity to convey a great sense of nautical satisfaction. This style is also seen increasingly in the many landscapes that he now produces.

Frank Shipsides retains his contacts with the Bristol Savages. A writer was once asked to to explain the popularity of the Savages and the so-called Savage spirit. It was, he replied, 'a shared love of the arts, good conversation and a warm sense of comradeship with one's fellow beings'. It would be difficult to find a more apt description of Frank Shipsides.

# The Illustrations

***A Severn trow in the Bristol Channel***

A Severn trow passes a square rigger in the Bristol Channel. The open hull of the trow and the canvas sides made it vulnerable to heavy seas when down-channel. Trows went as far up-river as Bridgnorth and the last one ceased trading in 1931.

*The Royal Barge at the opening of the Maritime Heritage Centre*

The royal barge on the Floating Harbour with
H.M. Queen Elizabeth and Prince Philip aboard at
the opening of the Maritime Heritage Centre.
Friday, 26 July, 1985.

*Evening on the waterfront*

The waterfront at eventide when the impact of soft light on the water creates an unforgettable impression. The Bush warehouse behind now houses the Arnolfini Gallery.

*Looking down Welshback*

Looking down Welshback, the traditional quay in the harbour for trade with Wales.

*The* **Harry Brown** *at Hotwells*

Named after the founder of a well-known Bristol dockside dynasty, the ship was a sand sucker, seen here fully loaded and homeward bound.

*Hill's* Boston City

The City Docks in their heyday. The Bristol City Line's *Boston City* is seen discharging cargo from New York between the wars.

*Evening at Clevedon*

Evening at Clevedon, on the North Somerset coast. The Victorian pier has been recently restored and is a regular calling point for the p.s. *Waverley* and m.v. *Balmoral*. It was the favourite pier of Poet Laureate John Betjeman.

*Midday light*

*The* Balmoral *and* Scillonian II *at the Grove*

The Bristol excursion company P. & A. Campbell often laid their ships up in the City Docks, and *Balmoral* does so each winter to this day. St Mary Redcliffe is beyond.

*The Cathedral from Prince Street Bridge*

The Cathedral was founded as St Augustine's Abbey and much of it dates from the fourteenth century. However, it was not completed until Victorian times.

**Campbell's** Ravenswood

P. & A. Campbell's paddle steamer *Ravenswood* as she appeared when built in 1891. She served an incredible sixty-four years, including two periods as a R.N. minesweeper, and only went for scrap in 1954.

**H.M.S. Flying Fox** *moving off*

The old frigate served Bristol naval volunteers from 1923 when she was first moored at Mardyke wharf until Sunday, 18 March, 1973, when the R.N.V.R. moved ashore.

*The Pill ferry ticket office*

The ferry crossed the Avon from the pilot village of Pill to the Bristol suburb of Shirehampton, and is celebrated in the song 'Old Pill Ferry Ride' by Adge Cutler and the Wurzels. The Lamplighters Inn at Shirehampton is behind.

**Britannia** *in the Bristol Channel*

Campbell's paddle steamer, *Britannia*, flagship of the fleet from 1896 and most popular with trippers, is seen passing the *Archibald Russell* in the Bristol Channel.

*Square rigger in the Channel with banana boat*

A square rigger in the Channel with one of Elders and Fyffe's numerous banana boats. Bristol was a major banana port for most of the twentieth century.

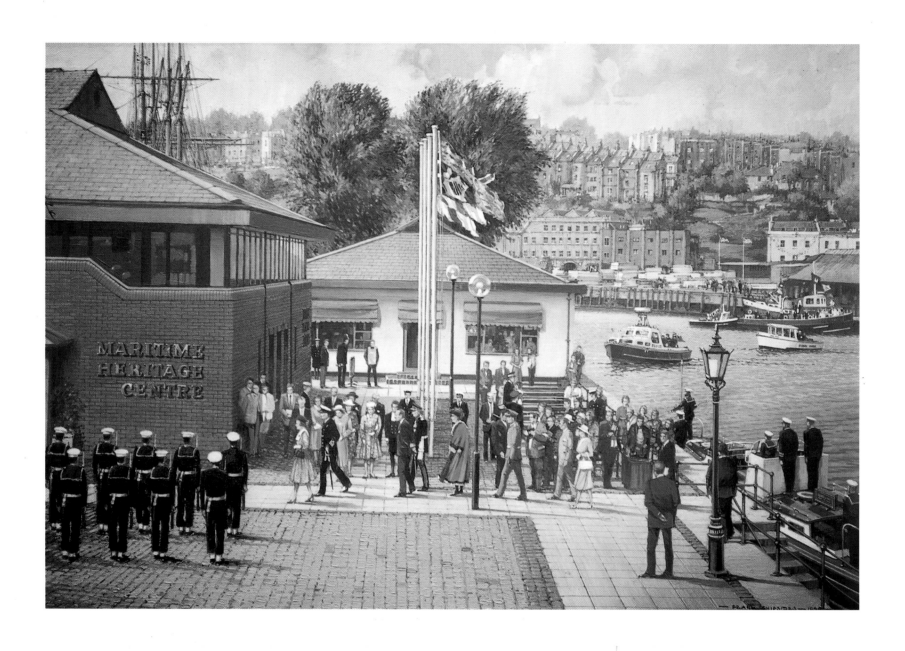

H.M. Queen Elizabeth II at the opening of the
Maritime Heritage Centre in 1985.

*Elder and Fyffe's* Ariguani *leaving Avonmouth*

Elders and Fyffe's *Ariguani* leaving Avonmouth, outward
bound for the Caribbean and another cargo of bananas.

*Avonmouth Docks*

Avonmouth Docks were first opened at the mouth of the river in 1877 and much enlarged between 1902–08.

**The** Formidable

The training ship *Formidable*, moored in Kingroad from 1869 to 1906 is passed by the pilot cutter *Marguerite*. *Formidable* was replaced by Portishead Nautical School.

*The* **Sand Diamond** *in the Cumberland Basin*

Tom Silvey's sand dredger *Sand Diamond*, seen here in Cumberland Basin, was one of the last working boats to operate in the City Docks.

*Shipping on the Avon*

The navigation of the river, with its bends and mudbanks was a tricky business and pilotage was obligatory, as the huge tidal range was fatal to the unwary.

*The opening of the Royal Edward Dock*

The opening of the Royal Edward Dock by King Edward VII on board the Royal Yacht *Victoria and Albert* on 9 July, 1908.

*The* Danmark *at Avonmouth*

The Danish training ship *Danmark* on a courtesy visit to Avonmouth, to celebrate the 600th anniversary of county status.

*Last of an era* – Flying Fox

Last of an era. *Flying Fox*, the R.N.V.R. drill ship moored in Bristol from 1923 to 1973 and was a firm favourite with naval reservists. A sad Sunday evening for Bristol shiplovers.

*High tide on the river*

High tide on the river, from the 2001 Bristol Savages
Annual Exhibition. The scene is typical of the years
before the First World War.

*Entrance to Ashton Court*

The entrance to Ashton Court Mansion, ancestral home of the Smythe family which was acquired for the people of Bristol in 1958 and was restored as a suite of assembly rooms.

*Stratford Mill, Blaise*

Stratford Mill, a restored corn mill on the Blaise Castle estate in north Bristol.

**The Passat, *the last of the Cape Horners to visit Bristol***

The *Passat* at Avonmouth on 12 October, 1948. She was the last large sailing ship to deliver a commercial cargo of Australian grain to the port of Bristol.

*Through the bridge, Redcliffe*

Redcliffe Backs, seen through Redcliffe Bridge, was a centre of the grain trade. It was closed in the early '80s.

*The Victoria Rooms*

The Victoria Rooms at Clifton, designed by Charles
Dyer and built 1838-42 as a set of assembly rooms,
which were later acquired by Sir George Alfred Wills
as headquarters of the University Union.  Today they
house the University music department.

*The Red Lodge*

The Red Lodge, given to the city in 1920 by the Bristol Savages and today a museum on Park Row. The building houses the Wigwam, permanent home of the Savages.

*Westbury College*

Westbury College, restored by William Canynges in the fifteenth century. Prince Rupert used it as a headquarters for the siege of Bristol in 1643 and demolished it when he evacuated the city, so that the building in College Road is all that remains of a large monastic foundation.

*Westbury Church*

Westbury-on-Trym parish church. Fifteen hundred
years ago, an early Saxon church on the site was was
sacked by Vikings who sailed up the then much
larger River Trym.

*John Wesley's statue*

John Wesley's statue stands outside the New Room in Broadmead, the first Methodist chapel in the world. The statue dates from 1932.

58

*The* **Strathmore** *at Avonmouth*

A visiting P. & O. liner *Strathmore* at Avonmouth in 1937.  Cruise ships still call occasionally.

*Ashton Court Mansion*

Ashton Court Mansion lies in the heart of a beautiful estate on the south side of the city. Long the home of the Smythe family, it is today a favourite spot for Bristolians.

*The Assembly Rooms, Clifton*

The Assembly Rooms, Clifton, dating from 1811, are by Bristol architect Francis Greenway, who was transported for forgery and became the father of Australian architecture. Today the building is the home of the Clifton Club.

*Blaise Chapel*

The Blaise Castle Estate at Henbury has several
buildings that attract interest.

*The Lord Mayor's Chapel*

The Lord Mayor's Chapel, St Mark's, came into civic ownership at the Dissolution in 1549, and remains the only municipal owned church in England.

*The Severn Bridge*

The Severn Bridge, opened in 1966, and first of two crossings of the Severn to be built north of the city. There are 3240 feet of decking between the main piers.

*Clifton Suspension Bridge from Sion Hill*

Clifton Suspension Bridge from Sion Hill. First
proposed in 1753, it was designed by I. K. Brunel in
1830 and finally opened in December, 1864. It is the
city's trademark and all Bristol knows that the bridge
is 702 feet long and 290 feet above the river bed.

*Evening cruise*

P. & A. Campbell's post-war flagship *Bristol Queen* (1946-67) returning up the Avon from an evening cruise.

*H.M.S.* Bristol *at Avonmouth*

H.M.S. *Bristol* at Avonmouth. The seventh R.N. ship to carry the name of the city, the ship was a regular visitor to the city during the 1980s and 1990s.

*Ashmead's tugs* – **Benfleet** *and* **Thelmliegh**

Ashmeads was one of a number of tug and lighter companies that prospered in the port during its heyday.

*Hotwells, early 1920s*

Hotwells in the early 1920s. The name derives from a famous Georgian spa which later became polluted.

*Royal West of England Academy*

The Royal West of England Academy building in Queens Road dates from 1858. The Academy was granted a Royal Charter by King George V in l913 and its present title dates from that year.

*Corner of Clare Street*

A corner of Clare Street, in the heart of the old city, and named after Lord Clare who was M.P. for Bristol from 1754. The parish church of St Stephen's.

*Memories of the market*

Memories of the market. The traditional wholesale
market moved to St Philip's in 1968 but market
activities abound still in the old site
near St Nicholas Street.

*Sea Mills*

Sea Mills, well known mid-point on the passage to the sea and site of the river signal station.

*Broad Street*

Broad Street, entered by the archway of St John on the Wall, contains the splendid Victorian Grand Hotel and on its corner with Corn Street is Sir Robert Smirke's Old Council House, now used as law courts.

*St Michael's Hill*

St Michael's Hill takes its name from the church of
St Michael's on the Mount Without and was one the
first streets in Bristol to develop outside the city walls.

*The* Marques *and* Inca, *St Augustine's Reach*

The training ships *Marques* and *Inca* lying in St Augustine's Reach. Bristol has been a favourite haven for such vessels but both the ships seen here met untimely ends.

*St Mary on the Quay and Colston's statue*

St Mary on the Quay, designed by R. S. Pope, was purchased by the Catholic Church in 1843 and has an impressive Corinthian portico. The quay has long disappeared under the modern roadway. Across the road is the statue of the Bristol philanthropist Edward Colston by Cassidy erected in 1895. Colston's connections with the slave trade remain controversial.

*Bristol Cathedral*

Bristol Cathedral's fourteenth century choir, with three alleyways of equal height, is unique among English cathedrals and is of great architectural interest. The nave and west front are Victorian structures by G. E. Street.

*Park Street, looking up*

Looking up Park Street, which dates from the late Georgian era. The top is dominated by the great Gothic tower of the University of Bristol's Wills Memorial Building which was designed by Sir George Oatley and completed in 1925. It is perhaps Bristol's best known building. The Council House by Vincent Harris is on the left.

*Blaise Hamlet*

Blaise Hamlet was built by the Harford family who
owned Blaise Mansion. Now owned by the National
Trust, the group of ten cottages was designed
by John Nash and built in 1811.

*The Festival of the Sea*

The Festival of the Sea was held in the City Docks in the summer of 1996, to herald the 500th anniversary of Cabot's voyage to America in 1497. The ship is the U.S. frigate *Rose*.

86

*Moorings*

St Mary Redcliffe and Redcliffe Parade dominate the upper reaches of Bristol Floating Harbour.

*St George's and the Cabot Tower*

St George's Church and the Cabot Tower on Brandon
Hill. The church dates from the Georgian era and is
now a successful concert hall. The Cabot Tower was
built in 1897-98, to a design of W. V. Gough to celebrate
the 400th anniversary of Cabot's American voyage.

*Returning home, the S.S.* Great Britain

The S.S. *Great Britain* on passage back to Bristol in 1970. The view from the Somerset bank.

*The return of the S.S.* **Great Britain**

Brunel's grand old ship passes under Brunel's Suspension Bridge on the morning of Sunday, 5 July, 1970. The riverbanks were lined with thousands of cheering Bristolians.

*Tall ships days*

P. & A. Campbell's Glen Usk (right) returning from a cruise.

*The* Wanderer *at Hotwells*

Immortalised by the poet John Masefield, who served in her, *Wanderer's* main skysail yard made her the 'tallest' ship to enter the City Docks.

*Christmas in King Street*

Christmas in King Street, home of Bristol's Theatre
Royal which dates from 1766 and is the oldest working
theatre in the country. The street also has the
half-timbered Llandoger Trow inn, built in 1664.

*Corn Street*

Looking along Corn Street, with its Georgian buildings, ancient churches, and the famous nails, origin of the phrase 'cash on the nail'.

96

*Bristol Bridge*

Bristol Bridge was rebuilt in 1768 and has remained largely unchanged since. Previous to 1768, the bridge carried houses, shops and a church, in the manner of old London Bridge.

*Bristol and Clifton Golf Club – the 13th hole*

Such is Bristol's rural location, this attractive scene is scarcely a mile from the city centre.

*Bristol and Clifton Golf Club – the Clubhouse*

*A Gilbert and Sullivan Medley*

This picture shows a miscellany of Savoy Opera characters, inspired by the artist's long association with the Bristol Catholic Players.

*The first voyage of the S.S.* Great Britain

The first voyage of the S.S. *Great Britain,* from an oil painting which shows the ship as she was in 1844 with six masts. The incomplete Suspension Bridge is behind.

**Cavina** *and* **Bristolian**

Tugs were a permanent feature of the harbour scene.

*As she was in 1848 – the S.S.* Great Britain

The S.S. *Great Britain* as she was in 1848, after alterations following going aground on the Irish coast. This picture should be compared with that on page 102.

*Frenchay Church*

Frenchay Church in verdant South Gloucestershire, famous for its association with Dr W. G. Grace.

*St Mary Redcliffe*

St Mary Redcliffe and its spire dominates central Bristol. The great medieval church, rebuilt by Canynges in the fifteenth century, is one of the finest parish churches in England.

*King Street with a glimpse of St Thomas's and the Lightship*

A glance along King Street to St Thomas' Church across
the harbour and the Lightship, preserved as a pub!

*Corn Street (winter evening)*

A winter evening in Corn Street, looking towards Christ Church.

*The* **Danmark** *– off Avonmouth*

The training ship *Danmark* off Avonmouth in the Kingroad.

**Fisherman at Saltford**

The peace and tranquillity of the Avon attracts a fisherman at Saltford between Bristol and Bath.

*Clifton College*

Clifton College with its fine collection of Gothic-style buildings, was founded in 1862 and soon grew into one of England's finest public schools. Here on the cricket field, Dr Grace led Gloucestershire to the County Championship, and in 1899, A. J. Collins scored 628 not out, which remains the highest ever score. He took five afternoons to do it.

*High tide, Pill*

A high tide on the Avon at Pill, the traditional
home of Bristol pilots.

*Moorings at Pill*

The moorings at Pill haven.

*Redcliffe Backs*

Redcliffe Backs in the City Docks.

*The garden, Florence Park*

The artist's garden at Florence Park in Bristol.

*Toward Welshback over Bristol Bridge*

In the medieval era, this was the area used by the ships from Wales.

*The* Matthew *in the Cumberland Basin*

This replica of Cabot's ship was built on Redcliffe Wharf in Bristol to celebrate the 500th anniversary of Cabot's 1497 voyage. She crossed the north Atlantic in the summer of 1997 and arrived in Buonavista, Newfoundland on 24 June.

*Foggy day, Cumberland Basin*

A foggy day in Cumberland Basin, gateway
to the City Docks. Fog in the river often held
up ship movements in the days before the
invention of radar.

*The* Matthew *at the Festival of the Sea*

The *Matthew* at the Festival of the Sea in 1996, p.s. *Waverley* is on the right.

*The* Annan *at St Augustine's Reach*

The *Annan* at St. Augustine's Reach, which was first excavated from 1240 to 1247. The Sloan line ran from Bristol to Belfast and Glasgow.

*The* Kaskalot *with the S.S.* Great Britain

The *Kaskalot* is a regular visitor to Bristol. It is a successful charter operator, and is now based in Cornwall.

126

*Wickham Bridge*

Wickham Bridge in the Frome valley. A preserved packhorse bridge, it was used by Cromwell to carry his Ironsides into Bristol, during the seige of 1645.

128

*From the Sea Walls*

The fine vista from the Sea Walls, looking up-river from the sea.

*Queen Square*

Queen Square, one of Bristol's glories, dates from the
reign of Queen Anne and was laid out on the old city
Marsh.  It contains Rysbrack's statue of William III, one
of the finest equestrian statues in the country.

***The Three Churches***

The three churches, part of Bristol's famous skyline. St Nicholas, All Saints and Christ Church from Welshback.

*The* Lord Nelson

The training ship *Lord Nelson*, on a visit to Bristol.

*Clare Street, looking up*

Looking up Clare Street, the office quarter of the old
city, although many businesses have relocated to cheaper
premises in the suburbs.

*The* Balmoral

The motor vessel *Balmoral*, an excursion vessel dating from 1948, is a preservation project based in Bristol and a familiar sight in the City Docks.

*Clifton Cathedral*

The striking Roman Catholic Cathedral of St Peter and St Paul at Clifton, which opened in the 1970s, is made from modern materials to a hexagonal design which has proved to be successful.

*Concorde*

Concorde taking off from Filton airfield. In the background is the Assembly Hall by Eric Ross, which dates from 1948. The great supersonic aeroplane has always been a source of pride in Bristol.

**The Britannia *at Portbury***

The Royal Yacht *Britannia* at the opening of Royal Portbury Dock. The yacht made three visits to Bristol during her career.

*The weir at Saltford*

The weir on the Avon at Saltford – a scene of peaceful
tranquillity not far from the city.

*Autumn glory, Christ Church, Clifton*

# Acknowledgements

❧❧❧

The artist and author are grateful for the generous assistance of many people in the preparation of this book, and in particular to Peter Slade, partner in Alexander Gallery, Bristol for recommending and locating the pictures that appear in the book.

They also thank the following for permission to use pictures in their possession:-

Mrs Chris Brisbane, Monsignor J. Buckley, Mr and Mrs John Harris, Mr and Mrs Michael Hodder, Mrs Connie Morgan, Veronica and Angela, Mr and Mrs Keith Morris, Miss May McMillan, Mr and Mrs Robin Sylvester, Mr and Mrs Pat Shipsides, Mr Mark Taylor, Mr and Mrs Pat Thwaites, Mr and Mrs Joe Woodbridge, the Bristol and Clifton Golf Club and Bristol City Council.

The artist and author are also grateful to Steven Pugsley and his staff at Halsgrove for much help and good advice, and to their own families for that support which the production of another book entails.

**Frank Shipsides  Robert Wall** – *Bristol 2001*